Where The Light Finds Me

A Journey Through Pain, Peace, and Purpose

Where The Light Finds Me

A Journey Through Pain, Peace, and Purpose

SAGAR MONDAL

B!gfoot Publications
Because, there's a writer in everyone.
INDIA
MALAYSIA
UNITED KINGDOM

Bigfoot Publications
Because, there's a writer in everyone.

Where The Light Finds Me
Author: Sagar Mondal
Cover Designer: Anze Ban V.
Illustrator: Bharat Karade

First Published by:
Bigfoot06 Publications (OPC) Pvt. Ltd.
1st floor, BSR Building near Vishal Mega Mart,
Daultabad Flyover, Laxman Vihar Phase 3,
Gurugram, Haryana (122001)
Website: www.bigfootpublications.in
Email: info@bigfootpublications.in

First Edition: January, 2025

ISBN Print Book: 978-93-6347-024-8

Printed in India.

Preface

Where The Light Finds Me is more than a collection of poetry; it's a personal journey through the complex emotions that come with love, loss, and the slow rediscovery of self.

The pieces within these pages aren't limited by gender—they're for anyone who has ever been touched by love's beauty and its pain. You may find in these pages a mirror for your own emotions or perhaps a guide to help illuminate a way forward.

As you move through these words, I hope that these words find you wherever you are and remind you that, though the journey may be difficult, there is always light waiting to meet *you*.

"Don't grieve. Anything you lose comes round in another form."

- Rumi

Contents

The Day I Found You

You didn't walk in;
you arrived—
like the first breath of spring
after a long winter.

The room stilled,
my thoughts blurred,
and in that moment,
you became the only thing
I wanted to see.

You carried a colour with you,
one I couldn't name—
soft but vivid,
gentle but unmissable.

It painted everything around me,
until the world felt brighter
just because you were in it.

We lay on the grass,
the stars stretching endlessly above us.

"This feels infinite," you said,
your voice soft in the dark.

I looked at you instead of the sky,
because in that moment,
you were the only thing
that felt like forever.

We didn't rush;
we lingered,
letting the space between us
fill with quiet smiles,
unspoken questions,
and the first threads
of something we couldn't yet name.

Falling for you felt like finding myself—
like finding a hidden garden
tucked away in a city's corner,
its colours too vibrant to ignore.

I walked into that garden slowly,
touching its petals,
knowing I had stumbled upon something rare,
something that would grow
only if I stayed.

That night, we walked together,
our steps falling into sync.

The streetlights flickered,
casting shadows
that seemed to entwine like us.
I wanted to hold your hand,
but I didn't—
afraid of breaking the fragile magic
of our first walk home.

It wasn't the conversations,
or the laughter,
or even the shared stories.

It was the silence between us—
not heavy,
but full of comfort,
like we had known each other
long before we met.

You were like a song I had forgotten,
a melody that suddenly came back—
familiar, comforting,
making me wonder
how I ever lived
without it.

Our love began like a tiny flame,
fragile, flickering,
but warm enough to hold close.

I cupped my hands around it,
afraid the wind would take it—
not realising
that one day,
it would burn out,
not from the wind,
but from the quiet absence
of your hands.

We stood under an awning,
the rain pouring around us.

"Run or wait?" you asked,
a laugh in your voice.
I chose to stay,
because I knew
I'd rather stand in one place forever
than risk missing another second
with you.

You see the small things—
the crack in the pavement
that forms a heart,
the way the leaves tremble
before the wind arrives.

You once noticed
a thread loose on my sleeve,
your fingers fixing it without a word.

It's the way you see
what others miss,
as if the world speaks to you
in whispers.

I once tried to describe you to a friend.
"She's like..." I began,
but I couldn't find the words.

You were too many things:
the calm of a morning breeze,
the warmth of sunlight on bare skin,
the colour of autumn leaves
caught in motion.

I realised then
that you weren't something to be described.
You were something to be felt,
known in silence,
cherished without explanation.

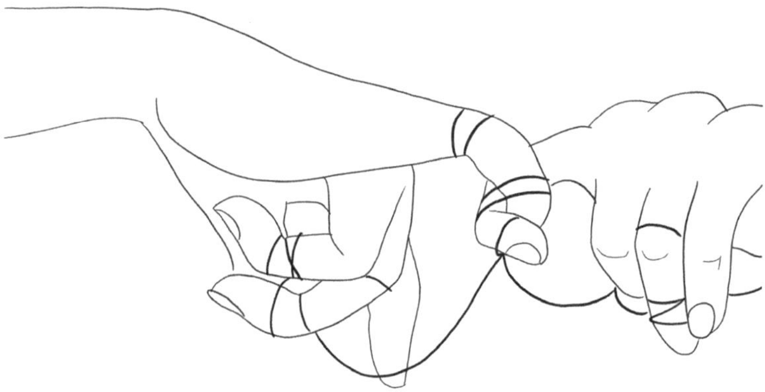

Between The Lines

We spoke a language only we knew,
written in glances,
woven through laughter,
etched in the spaces
where our fingers intertwined.

It felt endless,
like we'd always understand each other,
even when no words were spoken.

You always drank your coffee lukewarm,
letting it sit for too long.

I teased you about it,
handing you the cup
before it had the chance to cool.

You'd laugh, saying,
"Maybe I like it better this way."
I thought it was just coffee.
I didn't see then
how you liked everything
to feel easy.

We started a song together—
a melody we loved,
hummed softly in the evenings.

But one day,
I realised I was singing alone,
your voice fading into silence,
your tune forgotten
as mine stumbled
to find its way.

You didn't notice the small things—
the way I folded your favourite blanket,
or how I brought you tea
without being asked.

And I didn't say anything,
thinking that someday,
you would see.
But the moment passed,
and you didn't.

You had a way of staying quiet,
letting my words fill the room,

I didn't notice at first.
I thought you liked to listen,
that my voice was enough.

But now I wonder
if you stayed silent
because you had nothing
to say.

Our love was like a picture frame,
tilted slightly on the wall.

It didn't seem like a big deal—
just a small adjustment,
an easy fix.

But every time I passed it,
I noticed.
And every time you didn't,
the tilt grew heavier.

You promised we'd watch the stars together,
but when the night came,
you were tired.

I sat by the window,
looking up at the sky alone,
telling myself
it was just one night.
But promises, like stars,
are meant to shine.
And yours didn't.

You gave me a flower once,
but you never watered it.

I tried to keep it alive,
to nurture it with my hands.
But love, like flowers,
can't survive
on one person's care.

There's a space between the lines
of every story we shared—
the words unsaid,
the pauses heavy with meaning.

In those spaces,
I still find you.
Not in the laughter,
not in the endings,
but in the quiet in-between,
where our hearts spoke
without sound.

It's strange,
how I remember those silences
as clearly as the words,
as if the things we didn't say
told the truest story of all.

You didn't say thank you
when I stayed up late for you,
or when I made space for your dreams.

I didn't notice at first.
But one day,
it hit me like a wave—
you never asked for these things,
but you also never cared
to see them.

It was our special day of the year,
and you forgot.

I told myself you were busy,
that you'd remember later.
But later never came.

I smiled through it,
pretending it didn't matter,
but that was the first time
I wondered if I mattered to you
at all.

You sat across from me,
your eyes distant,
your words too few.

I tried to hold the moment together,
tried to weave us back
into something whole.
But the threads unraveled,
and you let them fall.

I didn't know it then,
but that was the last night
we'd ever share.

You never said goodbye—
just faded,
like a sunset that slipped
into the night too quickly.

I waited for a closure,
for a reason,
for anything
to make sense of the silence.

But you gave me none,
and I was left
to close the door myself.

There's a kind of ending
that doesn't come with words.
It comes with absence,
with the space someone leaves behind.

I wanted closure,
wanted to hear you say
that it mattered,
that I mattered.

But instead,
you disappeared into the quiet,
leaving me with nothing
but questions.

The Weight Of Goodbye

The air is different now,
thick, weighty, like dusk before rain,
and I wait, in the silence,
for something to break this ache.

Our love was like a book half-read,
the story left untold,
pages unfinished, words fading—
a tale I may never know the end of.

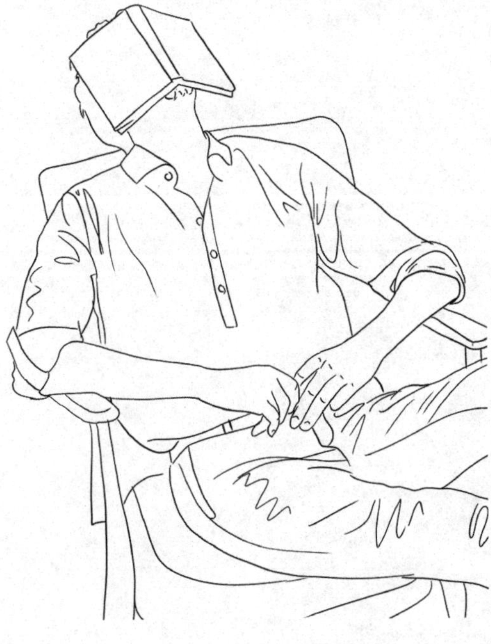

Every morning, I made two cups of tea.
One for you, one for me.
And when you left, I kept on making two,
as if you might return to drink it.
Weeks passed before I noticed
the second cup, cold and untouched.
I realised—
I'd been holding onto a seat
you were never coming back to fill.

I reach for you in dreams,
finding only shadows
where once your warmth was real,
and I wake, hollowed and alone.

There were so many things
I never got to say—
words I practised
in the dark of my mind,
hoping they'd somehow reach you.

But silence found a home
where sentences should be,
and now,
these unsent words gather dust,
like letters never mailed.

Once, I found an old key in the back of a drawer. I couldn't recall what it opened, only that it was important at some point. Today, I hold memories of us like that key—knowing they held meaning, but the lock they opened is gone. I let it slip back into the drawer, letting it remain a mystery, much like what we once were.

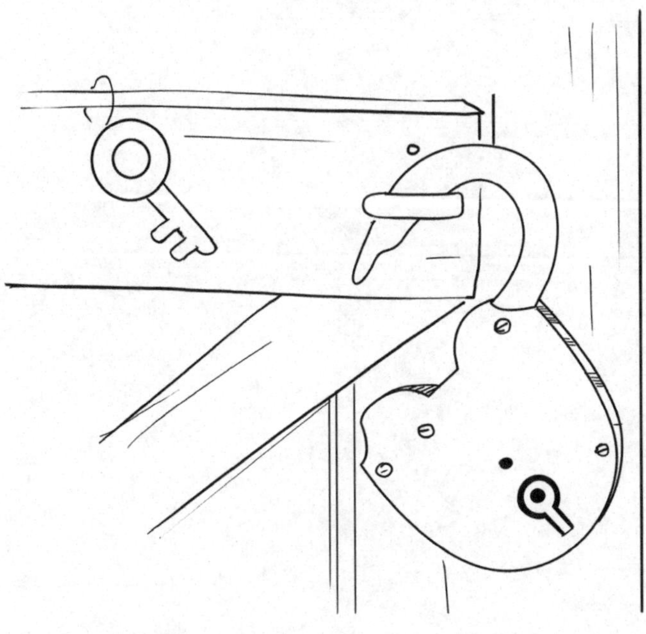

There's a way you laugh,
like you're letting the whole world in
on a secret only we know.

I watch you, across the room,
your shoulders lifting,
your eyes shining like small stars.

In those moments,
the room feels smaller,
like it's just you and me
and nothing else matters.

In every quiet room,
I still hear the echoes of us—
our laughter, our whispers,
the sound of your name
lingering on my breath.

Sometimes, I think I catch a glimpse of you,
in a crowded café or passing by.
But it's just the echo,
another memory refusing to fade.

The nights are endless now,
dark stretching into dark,
where sleep is a stranger,
and dreams are haunted by you.

I close my eyes,
and you're there,
alive in fragments,
haunting like a song
I can't quite forget.

I found the jigsaw puzzle we started together,
its pieces scattered, half-finished.
We had laughed at its difficulty,
promised we'd see it through.

But now, I realise it's just fragments,
incomplete and abandoned.
Some puzzles, like some people,
aren't meant to be finished.

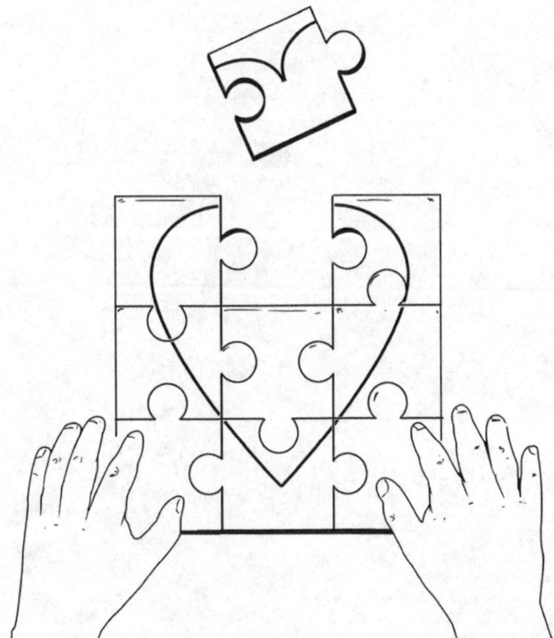

There's a space where you used to be,
a hollow shape that fits only you.
I've tried to fill it—
with books, with music, with busy hands—
but it's stubborn,
this empty space.

I sit beside it sometimes,
wondering if time will soften its edges,
or if I'll carry it with me,
a part of you stitched into my quiet places.

It's not the presence of things
that hurts the most.
It's the absence.
The way your laugh isn't here,
how empty the room feels
without the sound of you.

Love was our garden,
but we forgot to tend it.
Now, wild things have taken root,
weeds growing over the places
we once nurtured with care.

I stand there, looking at it all,
knowing I can't go back,
can't pull each weed out by hand.
Some gardens are better left as they are,
a lesson buried in the soil.

Your hand fits in mine
as though they were made to hold each other,
palm against palm, fingers interlaced.
I trace circles on the back of your hand,
learning each curve, every line.

When we walk together,
I feel grounded,
like your hand is my anchor,
keeping me steady in a world
that's always moving too fast.

Loving you was like holding water in my hands—
cool, clear, slipping through my fingers,
no matter how tightly I tried to keep it.

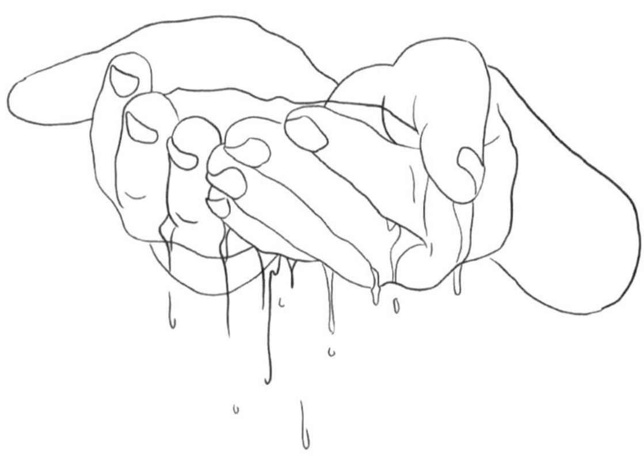

Your love was like rain on dry soil—
unexpected, nourishing,
but when it left,
it only made the cracks deeper.

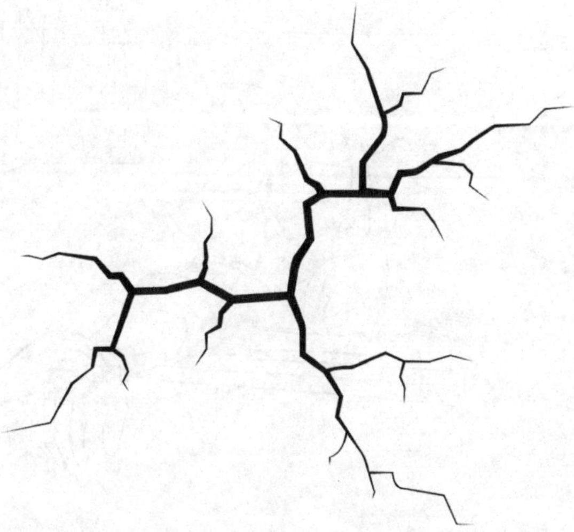

I walk through empty rooms,
your scent still lingering, faint,
like the trace of a dream,
lost as morning breaks.

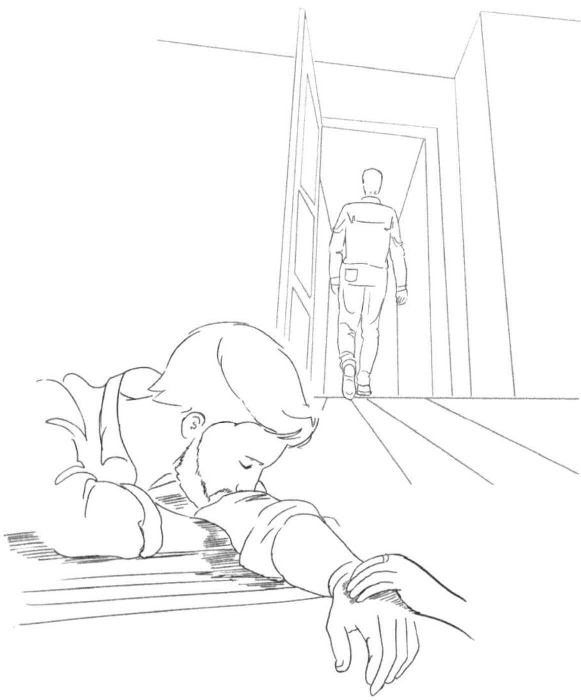

Goodbyes are like pouring tea
into a cup that isn't there—
the warmth spills,
but nothing holds it.

The more you try to fill it,
the more it pools around your feet,
soaking into the ground,
leaving only stains
where something whole should have been.

And yet,
we keep pouring,
hoping the cup will appear,
until we finally realise
it was never ours to hold.

It's the small things I love most—
the way you hum while cooking,
how you tuck loose hair behind your ear,
that slight crinkle in your nose
when you laugh too hard.

These moments are delicate,
like secrets you let me keep,
pieces of you
only I get to know.

Loving you was like chasing the horizon—
no matter how fast I ran,
you were always just out of reach.

In the mirror, I see shadows
of the person I was with you,
and I wonder if that reflection
will ever feel whole again.

In another life,
I think we're still walking side by side,
your laughter echoing through the streets,
your hand brushing mine.

Maybe we'd be different there,
finding each other all over again,
with no need for endings.

My memories of you
come in fragments now—
a laugh, a look,
the sound of your voice fading,
like shards of glass,
sharp but incomplete.

There was a song we loved,
one we played on quiet nights.
I heard it today, out of the blue,
and felt you there,
a shadow in the melody.

Funny how music holds memories
long after we let go.

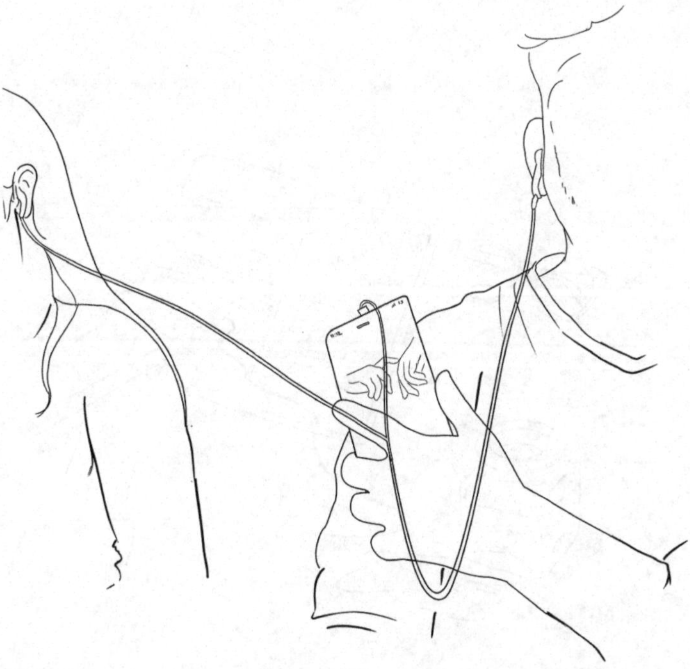

Our story stopped mid-sentence,
left unwritten, unfinished,
as if we'd run out of ink
or lost the will to write the end.

I wonder what it would be like
to hold your hand again—
to feel your warmth,
like sunlight reaching into the coldest places.

In this dream,
we don't say goodbye.
In this dream,
we're still writing our story.

You were a map I'd memorised,
knowing every curve, every line.
But now, as I trace those paths,
I find they lead nowhere,
a road I can't travel back on.

I pass by your street sometimes,
glancing at the window
where we once shared glances, laughter.

Now, it's just another street,
familiar but empty,
like a bookmark in a story
I've stopped reading.

If we were here now,
I'd tell you about the soft light
that falls on my window each morning,
how it reminds me of the way
you used to look at me.

We'd talk like nothing's changed,
like time hadn't scattered us.
Just you and me,
tangled in this quiet moment.

We've all waited at a station,
watching the trains arrive and depart.
Sometimes, we think one is meant for us,
its light shining in the distance,
its whistle carrying the promise of a journey.

But as it comes closer,
we realise—
its tracks veer in another direction,
its path not meant to merge with ours.

And so, we stand alone on the platform,
holding the weight of what could have been,
learning that not every train
will take us where we hoped to go.

The tracks remain,
but so do we—
ready to wait,
or perhaps to walk.

You're both known and unknown to me now,
a familiar stranger,
like a place I once lived in
but can no longer call home.

The clock on the wall stopped ticking
the day you left—
its hands frozen, unmoving,
caught in a moment of time
that refuses to pass.

Each day, I look at it,
wondering if I should set it right,
or leave it stopped,
a quiet reminder that time, too,
is sometimes stubborn with grief.

We lit a candle together,
its flame a warm promise.
Now, it sits cold and unlit,
a quiet reminder of light
we once shared
and chose to leave behind.

We walked this path so many times,
our footsteps leaving marks in the dirt.
Now, I walk it alone,
seeing only my tracks,
the trail of memories behind me.

We're like two boats
once anchored together,
but now drifting in opposite tides.

The water between us grows,
a distance too wide to bridge,
and I realise, painfully,
that some things can't be rowed back to shore.

We held each other for the last time,
not knowing it was the end.
Your arms were warm, steady,
like they always were,
and I held on,
too tightly, perhaps,
hoping to keep the moment.

But goodbyes are slippery,
slipping through hands,
like sand or water—
impossible to hold.

Shadows Of Memory

Memories hold a weight of their own,
heavier than I'd thought,
pressing into me on quiet nights,
their edges sharp,
their voices loud.

I try to tuck them away,
but they stay, stubborn,
etching themselves deeper,
unwilling to be forgotten.

I found a photograph of us, tucked away in an old book. We're laughing, eyes bright with the certainty of forever. I wanted to keep it, to remember us that way. But instead, I put it back in the book, closed the cover, and returned it to the shelf. Sometimes, memories are best left where you find them.

There's an old sweater of yours
at the back of my closet,
soft and fraying at the edges.

I can't bring myself to throw it out,
even though it no longer fits,
even though it only brings
a warmth of what was,
not what is.

You live in the corner of my mind,
a place where light meets shadow,
where memories sit in quiet rows,
fading, flickering, but still alive.

I don't visit often,
but sometimes, I linger,
knowing I might never leave.

There's a message I never sent,
left in drafts on my phone,
its words untouched, unsent,
like thoughts whispered to the wind.

Sometimes, I read it again,
letting the words fill my mind,
but I never hit "send,"
knowing some things
are meant to remain unsaid.

Our memories are like a glass jar,
filled with moments we sealed tight,
preserving laughter, glances,
the way you'd look at me.

But when I open it,
I realise they've faded,
like colours that lose their brilliance
when hidden from light.

There's a thin line between love and memory,
a place where past and present blur,
where feelings grow roots in forgotten soil.

I walk this line, knowing each step
takes me further from you
yet brings me closer
to the version of us
that lives in the shadows—
a place where we exist
without endings,
without loss.

You called me once,
long after the world had fallen asleep.

“I couldn’t wait until morning,” you said,
your voice breaking the stillness.
We talked about everything,
and nothing,
the way midnight always allowed.

Now, the night feels quieter,
as if it’s waiting
for the sound of you.

Some days, you feel close,
like a mirage on the horizon,
perfect yet unreachable.

I walk toward you,
hands stretched out to grasp,
but the closer I get,
the further you seem,
like something that was never real,
a trick of light and distance.

In my mind, you stay clear,
a vision I chase but never reach,
a memory that moves with me,
always just out of touch.

There's an old journal tucked away,
filled with fragments of us,
words we scribbled without thinking,
moments we captured to hold forever.

Now, the pages have yellowed,
edges worn, ink fading.
I flip through, skimming our words,
and realise that what once felt permanent
is slowly vanishing,
as all memories do.

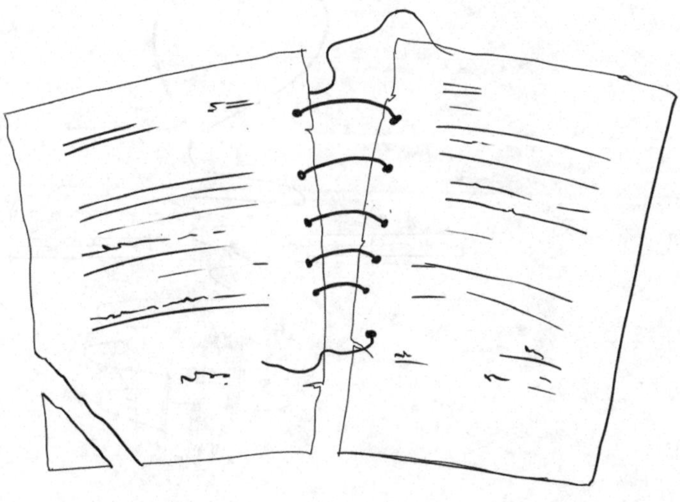

There's a feeling I don't know how to name,
something between sorrow and comfort,
like a song you once loved,
but can't bear to hear again.

It sits in my chest, this feeling,
heavy and quiet,
like a hand resting over my heart,
reminding me of something lost,
yet somehow beautiful.

There's an old clock in my room
that no longer ticks,
its hands frozen in place.

I keep it, though, as it is,
a silent witness to passing time,
as if, without its ticking,
time has no hold on it—
just like memories,
suspended in moments,
unaffected by the world moving on.

We built our love like a sandcastle,
each grain carefully placed,
each tower rising with promise.

But the waves came,
slow and steady,
erasing the edges,
until we stood on wet sand,
holding onto something
that was never meant to last.

There's a small café we used to visit on Sunday afternoons. I went back once, sat in the same corner, ordered the same coffee. It tasted different, as if your presence had been the secret ingredient all along. I haven't returned since; some places aren't meant to be revisited.

We were almost something beautiful,
almost whole,
but sometimes "almost"
is the closest you can get.

You and I were threads
meant to touch
but never truly weave,
two paths that crossed
but weren't meant to stay.

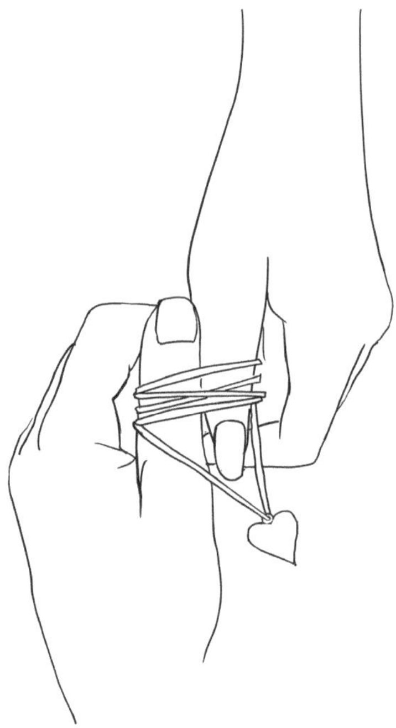

I keep a drawer locked tight,
filled with things that once held you—
notes scrawled in a rush,
a book you lent me,
small gifts that remind me your presence.

I don't open it anymore,
not out of fear,
but because I know some things
are meant to be kept hidden,
touched only by memory,
not by hands.

We were pieces of a puzzle,
close enough to fit,
but not quite right.

At first, we forced the edges,
trying to make them match,
ignoring the spaces that didn't fit.

But in the end,
a puzzle only works
when all its pieces belong.

We had a playlist, one we made together. After you left, I listened to it on repeat, each song a memory, each lyric a stitch in the fabric of us. Now, I've added new songs, ones that don't remind me of you. It's a strange feeling, like repainting a wall in the colour of forgetting.

Somewhere, you're laughing,
living, breathing,
and I wonder if you think of me
as much as I think of you.

Your memory is like a song I can't remember the words to—
the melody lingers, but the lyrics are gone,
and yet, I still hum it quietly.

You left your favourite book behind,
the one with dog-eared pages
and notes in the margins.

I opened it,
reading your thoughts
between the lines,
finding pieces of you
in every underline,
every quiet mark.

It felt like a conversation
we were still having.

We had a favourite road we used to walk down. I went back once, retracing each step, feeling the gravel crunch beneath my feet. But it felt empty without your hand in mine. I realised then that the road was just a road, a path to somewhere we never arrived.

I saw love as a promise,
one that meant forever,
a promise that would grow with us,
deepening, day by day.

You saw it as a season,
a thing to cherish,
but never to hold onto,
an experience, not a home.

There was once a lighthouse keeper
who lit his lantern every night,
guiding lost ships to safety,
though none ever came.

Yet each evening,
he'd climb those stairs,
light the flame,
and wait, alone,
hoping that tonight,
his light would mean something.

You wanted love like sunlight—
fleeting, warm,
a gentle glow that comes and goes.

I wanted love like the moon,
constant, reliable,
even in the darkest nights.

In the end, we drifted apart,
both of us drawn
to different lights.

A sailor lost at sea, looking for a shore that won't appear.
A prisoner imagining freedom through a window too small.
A bird singing to the dawn, not knowing the storm is near.
A river flowing towards a sea it will never reach.

We are made of wishes unfulfilled,
clinging to promises whispered but never kept,
hoping for things that slip through our fingers.

"What if" sits heavy in my mind,
a question with no answer,
a path not taken,
always out of reach.

We are all haunted by it,
the lives we didn't live,
the people we never became,
the roads that led somewhere else.

I sit on a bench where we once sat,
watching strangers pass,
all with their own lives,
their own memories and ghosts.

I wonder if this bench holds pieces of them,
a quiet witness to moments of laughter,
of tears, of silence.
A place doesn't belong to us alone—
it holds everyone who's ever stayed.

Memories taste bitter,
like coffee left too long.
I sip them slowly,
each one a familiar pang,
a taste I can't quite savour,
but can't bear to forget.

Our time together feels like a book
I've read too many times,
its pages worn, creased, familiar.
I turn each page,
knowing what comes next,
but reading it anyway,
reliving each word,
until the end feels close again.

I pass by an old house every day,
its windows broken,
walls weathered by years.
It feels haunted, but not by ghosts—
by memories of people
who loved there once,
who lived and lost,
leaving pieces of themselves
in every crack and crevice.

Some places linger with memory,
like cafes with empty seats,
parks with forgotten swings,
rooms filled with echoes.

We leave parts of ourselves there,
small offerings to the past,
a reminder that we existed,
even if just for a moment.

I've tried to forget you—
like erasing ink from paper,
but the marks remain,
faint shadows where words once lived.

I've folded the memories,
tucked them away in the quiet corners,
yet they unfold themselves,
softly, gently,
in the stillness of my mind.

It's not that I hold onto you—
it's that you linger,
like a melody I didn't ask to remember,
but can't seem to forget.

There are faces that remind me of you,
strangers with your smile,
people who move like you did.

I watch them,
holding onto the brief illusion,
pretending for a moment
that I've found you again.

The Mirror's Truth

I look back at us now
with clearer vision—
no longer bound by what I wanted to see.

I see the cracks, the missed chances,
the places where we both drifted.
I loved you deeply, yes,
but now I understand,
not everything deep
is meant to stay.

I read an old entry in my journal,
written in the thick of us.
I wrote of you in every line,
but I barely saw myself.
It's strange, reading it now,
realising how much space you took,
how little room was left for me.
I close the journal,
leaving those words behind,
ready to write something new.

I once thought the path forward
was one we'd walk hand in hand,
two steps in sync,
crossing the road together.
But now, I stand alone,
looking at the road ahead.
It's unmarked, unfamiliar,
but it's mine to walk,
and that feels enough.

Not all love is meant to stay;
some love teaches,
some love grows,
and some love leaves,
leaving lessons
that settle quietly
like dust on a windowsill.

There's a freedom now,
a lightness I hadn't known,
a space to breathe
without trying to fit into your world.

I find joy in the quiet,
in my own company,
a peace that feels like home.

I hold both sorrow and joy—
the memory of you still warm,
the reality of you now gone.

It's strange, this mixture,
a taste I can't describe,
a feeling that's both
heavy and light.

Today, I smiled without thinking of you,
a small, ordinary joy
in the middle of my day.

For a moment, I felt guilty,
as if I owed you my sadness,
but then I realised—
happiness belongs to me too.

My heart feels cautious,
wary of giving itself away.

But I find courage in small places—
a kind word, a friendly smile,
reminders that the world is gentle,
even if love has been hard.

I sat alone at a café,
ordered coffee just for me.
No need to share—
just my own company,
and it was enough.

For the first time,
silence felt full,
not of emptiness,
but of contentment.

I look at my own scars,
marks of the past I once tried to hide.

Now, I trace them gently,
each flaw a line in my story,
each scar a reminder
of battles won.

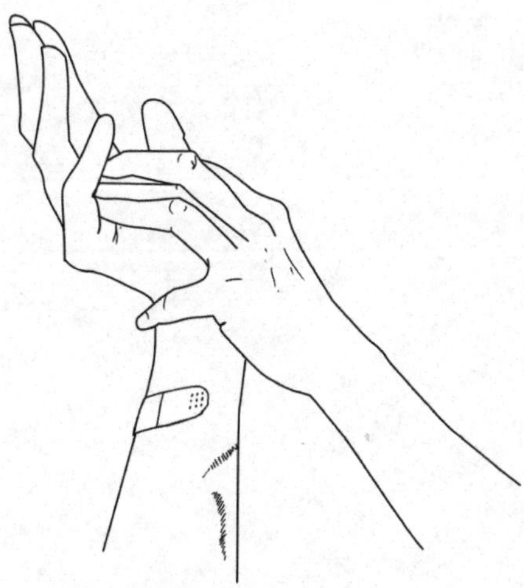

Piece by piece,
I gather parts of myself
I'd left behind,
the dreams, the voice,
the pieces I lost
while holding onto us.
I find myself again,
new and whole.

Goodbye brought me closer to myself,
led me to places I wouldn't have gone.

I hold no bitterness,
only gratitude,
for the person I am
because of, and beyond, you.

I noticed a flower bloom today,
its petals open and bright.
Once, I would have pointed it out to you,
shared the moment.
Today, I kept it for myself,
finding quiet joy
in the beauty of small things,
knowing I am enough to witness them.

Joy is a small thing—
a cup of tea, warm in my hands,
a breeze that lifts my hair,
a laugh shared with friends.
It's not grand,
but it's enough to remind me
that life moves on,
and so do I.

The love I gave you was real,
but maybe it was too much,
or perhaps it was exactly enough,
just not for you.

We talked once of dreams we'd chase together, plans made in half-whispers under moonlight. After you left, I looked at those dreams, wondering which were yours and which were mine. And there, in the quiet, I found that some dreams were meant to be mine alone.

Love is like planting seeds in soil;
sometimes, no matter how much we nurture it,
some things are simply not meant to grow.

You were a mirror,
showing parts of myself I didn't know,
and now that you're gone,
I'm left to find my reflection on my own.

I saw you today, across the street,
a glimpse of the person I once knew.
My heart skipped, then settled,
not with longing,
but with a calm acceptance.

You're familiar,
but now, only a stranger,
a reminder of who I used to be.

I find joy in the little things—
the smell of rain,
the taste of fresh tea,
the softness of a blanket
on a cold night.

Small, simple things,
reminding me that life's beauty
is here, in the present.

I don't have all the answers,
and maybe I never will.
But I find peace in that,
a freedom in the unknown,
learning to embrace the mystery
of life's unfolding.

We once sat by a train window,
watching the fields rush by,
your hand resting lightly on mine.

You spoke of places you wanted to see,
dreams you hadn't yet chased.
I listened, smiling,
thinking there'd always be time
to join you on those journeys.

Now, I see the same view alone,
but the fields look different,
as if they too know
that some journeys
we must take apart.

Love taught me strength—
not in holding tight,
but in learning to loosen my grip.

Letting go is pruning a tree,
where brittle branches fall away,
making room for green and bloom.

In letting go, I found a freedom
I had never chased,
and a quiet peace I had never known.

I thought I would break,
but here I am, stronger,
no longer defined by the love I lost,
but by the love I learned to give myself.

I am not what I lost,
nor what I held,
but all that I am becoming,
in the spaces in between.

There was a window we'd sit by, watching the world go by, talking of things we'd do together. Now, I sit alone, watching that same world. I realised that life goes on, with or without shared dreams. The view is the same, but I am different—stronger, wiser, and somehow, complete.

I used to carry the weight of it—
every mistake, every wrong turn,
every heartbreak.

Now, I forgive the past,
the person I was,
the choices I made.

I release it all,
letting it drift away
like leaves on a gentle breeze.

I am strong now,
but my strength isn't hard.

It's soft, like water,
flowing, moving,
finding its way
through every obstacle,
unbreakable in its grace.

There's a quiet confidence that grows
when you know yourself,
when you find strength
in your own company.

It's the kind of confidence
that doesn't shout, doesn't push—
it simply stands, steady, sure.
And in that stillness, I know:
I am enough,
whole and at peace,
ready for whatever comes next.

I thought the storm would break me,
but now, I see the flowers it left—
the resilience that sprouted,
the growth that took root
in the aftermath.

Every petal a reminder
that beauty can bloom
even from broken ground.

For so long,
I let my story intertwine with yours,
my pages filled with your words,
my chapters marked by your presence.
Now, I pick up the pen myself,
writing lines that are mine alone,
ready to tell my own story.

Now, I am free,
Finding way in the light of my own becoming.

Whispers Of Solitude

I used to fill every silence,
a rush to escape the empty spaces.

Now, I sit with quiet,
letting it settle, soft and calm,
like a blanket on a winter night
that asks nothing from me,
except to be here,
with myself.

Being alone is like learning a new language—
at first unfamiliar and difficult,
but soon, it flows naturally,
a voice you didn't know you had.

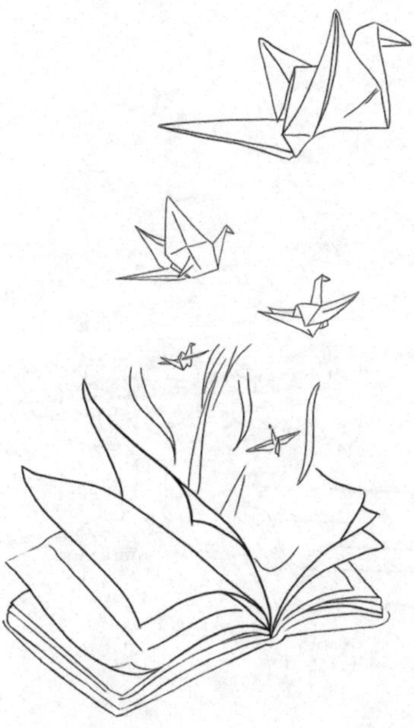

There's a strength in standing alone, I realise. Like a tree growing on a cliffside, roots gripping fiercely into the earth, holding itself upright. I am learning that my roots are stronger than I thought.

I spent so long searching for home
in others, in places,
in the spaces between.

But now, I feel it in myself,
a steady warmth,
a comfort I carry,
finding home in my own heart.

Solitude is like walking in a forest alone,
hearing only the sound of your own breath,
realising that you're part of a world bigger than yourself.

The silence once scared me,
an empty echo, hollow and cold.
Now, it feels like home,
soft, warm, mine.

Solitude is not loneliness;
it's a gift,
a chance to become our own best friends,
to know ourselves without the weight of expectation.
Alone, we can be whoever we want to be,
free from the mirrors of others.

Not every day asks for more.
Some days come softly,
inviting stillness,
asking only to be observed.

There is a beauty in quiet hours,
a gentle unfolding,
where time simply exists,
undisturbed.

I went to the park alone, watching people pass, couples holding hands, children laughing. I felt a pang of longing, but it faded as I sat on a bench, enjoying the breeze. I realised then that my presence here, alone and content, was enough. I didn't need to share this moment with anyone else.

Now it is like a quiet library,
rows of books untouched, waiting,
and each day, I am a new reader,
discovering chapters of myself.

Being alone feels like standing on the shore,
the vastness of the ocean stretching before you,
and realising the only waves that matter
are the ones you make for yourself.

In a pond undisturbed,
the water rests like glass,
reflecting sky,
mirroring trees,
keeping the world steady in its embrace.

No ripple breaks its surface;
even the air around it falls silent,
as if drawn into its spell.

A feather drifts on the wind,
unbound, untethered.
It doesn't fight the current;
it lets itself be carried.

There's no fear in its flight,
only trust—
that the breeze will take it
where it needs to go.

I set the table for one tonight,
no second plate, no extra chair.

At first, it felt wrong,
the space too big for just me.
But then, I savoured the quiet,
the way the meal tasted fuller,
the way the evening felt complete.

An empty cup isn't wasted.
It waits, patient and still,
knowing its time will come—
a moment to hold something new,
something meaningful.

There's beauty in its emptiness,
in the space it offers.

It's not emptiness I feel,
but openness—
a vast expanse within,
ready to be filled
not with another's presence,
but with my own.

In the stillness,
I relearn who I am—
the way I think,
the things I love,
the parts of me
that were quieted
by the noise of others.

A candle flickers,
its flame is small but steady.
It doesn't compete with the sun,
doesn't seek to brighten the world.

Its glow is quiet,
meant only to warm
the space it fills.

Today I boarded a train alone,
no one to talk to,
no one to plan for.

I thought I'd feel lonely,
but instead, I felt free—
each mile a quiet reminder
that this journey is mine,
and mine alone.

Alone doesn't mean lonely;
it means I have the space to hear myself,
to feel the rhythm of my heart,
to understand who I am
when the world is quiet.

There's grace in solitude,
a quiet dignity
that doesn't ask to be seen.

It moves like water,
soft and steady,
carving its path through the heart,
shaping it into something
stronger,
gentler,
whole.

The world moves fast,
but I don't need to.

I watch the sunrise,
the clouds shift,
the way the wind moves the trees.
In stillness,
I see everything
I once rushed past.

I thought love meant giving,
always giving,
until I had nothing left.

Now, I know it also means holding,
protecting the parts of myself
that deserve my own care.

I love myself enough
to stay whole.

It was raining the day we met—
soft droplets on your hair,
your laughter breaking through the storm.

You taught me to love the rain,
to dance in it,
to see the beauty in its chaos.

Even now,
when the sky darkens
and the clouds release their weight,
I find myself smiling,
thinking of that first rain
and how, for a while,
we both felt invincible.

The journey was long,
but here I am, whole and unbroken,
embracing the quiet,
and finding peace within.

Stepping Into The Light

There was a time
when the thought of you
felt heavy,
pressing into my chest
with every breath.

But today,
I feel only lightness,
like a bird taking flight.

You're still there,
not as a burden,
but as a breeze—
a gentle push,
helping me move forward
toward the sky.

Hope speaks softly,
a language I'm learning.
It's in the first sip of tea,
the softness of a sunrise,
the warmth of a familiar song.

I didn't notice it before,
but now,
I hear it everywhere.

Healing is like carrying a lantern
through a dark forest.

At first, it flickers,
barely enough to see ahead.
But with every step,
it grows brighter,
lighting the way
toward an open clearing.

Life feels like an old painting,
its colours once dulled by time.

But now, the restoration begins—
hues brightening,
details sharpening,
revealing a masterpiece
I hadn't fully seen before.

There's a bench in the park
I hadn't noticed before,
tucked beneath a tree
in full bloom.

I sat there today,
watching petals fall gently to the ground.
For the first time in years,
I felt content
with exactly where I was.

I used to fear the quiet, the blank spaces of my future. Now, I see them as canvas—empty, yes, but filled with possibility. I can paint this life as I wish, in colours I choose.

I am whole without seeking,
complete without needing,
walking with a quiet joy,
knowing I am enough.

To love is to let go, to be free,
and in that freedom, to return to myself—
a wanderer who has found home within.

There was a drawer I never opened,
filled with pieces of you:
a scarf, a note,
a photo from a summer day.

Today, I emptied it,
not with sadness,
but with a quiet smile.
I placed each item in a box,
not to discard,
but to set aside,
leaving space for the new.

What once felt like loss,
now feels like freedom.
What once weighed me down,
now lifts me, light as air,
carrying me into a sky wide open.

The puzzle we started remains unfinished,
but I've found my own pieces now—
ones that fit together
without needing yours.

The picture is different,
but it's mine,
and it's complete.

Life is a journey with no map, no fixed path. There are twists and turns, stops and starts. But in every moment, I am exactly where I need to be, and that is enough.

I’ve spent so long
searching for the light,
thinking it was somewhere
outside of me.

But now,
I see it’s always been here—
soft, steady,
burning quietly within,
ready to guide me
home.

Now, I walk forward,
not bound by the past,
but held by hope,
guided by a quiet faith,
that wherever I go,
I am Whole, I am *Free.*

Acknowledgements

This book would not exist without the love, patience, and support of those who have been by my side through every step of this journey. To my friends and family, who stood by me when words were my only way to process the world around me — thank you for believing in me.

To my readers, who inspire me to keep creating, your presence is a gift. And lastly, to those who have felt heartbreak, may you find comfort in these pages and know that you are not alone.